Original title:
Reclaiming Me

Copyright © 2024 Swan Charm
All rights reserved.

Author: Sabrina Sarvik
ISBN HARDBACK: 978-9916-79-054-0
ISBN PAPERBACK: 978-9916-79-055-7
ISBN EBOOK: 978-9916-79-056-4

Flames of My Inner Fire

In the shadows, embers glow,
A spark ignites, passion flows.
Flickering light, fierce and bright,
I stand tall, ready to fight.

Winds may blow, but I won't yield,
With every breath, my heart's my shield.
Through the storms, I chase the light,
Fueling the flames that burn so bright.

Chasing the Faintest Echo

Whispers dance on evening air,
Carried softly, beyond despair.
Each note lingers, a haunting plea,
In quiet corners, they call to me.

Through the mist, I seek their source,
Tracing echoes on a winding course.
Heartbeats quicken, shadows blend,
In search of voices that never end.

Embracing My Forgotten Whispers

Silent secrets from days of yore,
Hidden truths behind closed doors.
Fragile memories touch my heart,
In gentle echoes, they play their part.

Embrace the past, let it unfold,
Wisdom in whispers, stories told.
In forgotten corners, I find my song,
A melody sweet, I've yearned for long.

Journeying Through the Unseen

Paths uncharted, realms unknown,
With every step, my courage grown.
In shadows deep, I find my way,
Guided by dreams that lead astray.

The unseen whispers, soft and clear,
A symphony only I can hear.
Through tangled vines and misty night,
I journey forth towards the light.

The Light I've Always Carried

In shadows deep, I find my glow,
A warmth within, a steady flow.
Through darkest nights, it guides my way,
A beacon bright, come what may.

Through trials faced, its flame remains,
A whisper soft, it breaks my chains.
With every step, I learn to see,
The light within, it sets me free.

Sculpting My Identity

With every chip, I carve my soul,
A masterpiece, to make me whole.
The clay of dreams, I twist and mold,
In hands of fate, my truths unfold.

Each mark I leave speaks of my heart,
A journey where I play my part.
In every form, I find my voice,
In art I breathe, I make my choice.

Letting Go to Soar Higher

A heavy heart can weigh me down,
Yet I will shed the darkened crown.
With every tear, I learn to fly,
Unchain my spirit, spread my sky.

Released from fears, I rise above,
With open wings, I seek new love.
In letting go, I find my space,
To touch the stars, to embrace grace.

The Echo of My True Name

In silent halls, I hear the sound,
A whisper soft, where dreams are found.
It calls to me, a gentle ring,
The essence of my soul takes wing.

In every breath, it echoes clear,
A song of hope, I long to hear.
The name I speak brings peace within,
A melody where love begins.

The Dawn of My Resilience

In shadows deep, I find my way,
Each step I take, a brand new day.
Resilience blooms, though storms may roar,
I rise again, I will restore.

Hope whispers soft, in darkest night,
A gentle push, towards the light.
With every tear, a lesson learned,
A fire within, forever burned.

Mountains high, and valleys low,
My spirit grows, my courage glows.
Through trials faced, I stand so tall,
A warrior's heart, I will not fall.

The dawn arrives, a vibrant hue,
With every challenge, I breakthrough.
Embracing strength, I stand my ground,
In my own truth, I am found.

Steps Into My Own Light

Footprints marked on paths untold,
I walk with purpose, brave and bold.
Each moment lived, a fleeting chance,
To dance with life, to learn, to glance.

In shadows cast, I find my flame,
Reflections spark a glowing name.
From ashes rise, I greet the dawn,
With every step, my fears are gone.

I seek the sun, the skies so bright,
With open heart, I claim my right.
To shine my truth, in all I do,
Step by step, I break on through.

With every choice, I pave the way,
Into the light, I choose to stay.
A journey vast, a tale of might,
I walk, I run, in endless light.

Uncharted Waters of Reflection

Sailing forth on waves unknown,
The winds of change, they guide my own.
In depths of thought, I brave the sea,
With every swell, I learn to be.

The horizon calls with whispered dreams,
Through stormy nights, my courage beams.
Each wave a mirror, a look within,
I find my strength, I will begin.

The tides of time, they ebb and flow,
In quiet moments, I come to know.
With sails unfurled, I trust the glide,
In every heartache, I turn the tide.

Exploring depths where shadows lie,
I rise above, I shoot for the sky.
In uncharted waters, I find my voice,
In every wave, I make my choice.

A Glimpse into My Untold Stories

In shadows deep, my tales abide,
Whispers soft, where dreams confide.
Moments lost, but not in vain,
Time will weave them back again.

Pages blank, yet words ignite,
Hopes renew in the fading light.
Hidden truths shall find the way,
To tell their tales, come what may.

Through silent nights, the echoes call,
Each heartbeat writes, each rise and fall.
Memories dance in the misty air,
Glimpses shine, vibrant and rare.

Lifting veils, secrets unfold,
In every fear, there lies a bold.
Journey taken, paths divine,
In every story, I claim what's mine.

The Unfolding of Inner Light

In the stillness, the dawn will break,
Hearts ignite, for courage's sake.
Within the soul, a fire glows,
Transforming shadows into prose.

Silent wonders start to bloom,
Unraveling fears that once consumed.
Graceful steps on a path unknown,
Guided by light, seeds have sown.

Life's embrace, a gentle wave,
Leading us toward the brave.
In every tear, a lesson learned,
Through darkest nights, our spirits yearned.

Radiance spreads, a vibrant song,
Together, we become the strong.
With open hearts, we let love flow,
In a world where light can grow.

Writing My Own Narrative

With every pen stroke, dreams commence,
Crafting lines that break the dense.
Chapters written in a heartfelt tone,
Each word a step, not alone.

Beneath the weight, we hold our fate,
Ink reveals what we create.
In swirling thoughts, the visions thrive,
In every story, we derive.

Pages turn, a new dawn nears,
Transforming doubts into our cheers.
I pen the strength that fuels my soul,
Conquering fears to feel whole.

Lines of passion, lines of grace,
In every challenge, I find my place.
With every verse, my voice will soar,
Written truths that I adore.

The Phoenix Rising from Within

Through the ashes, hope will rise,
A flicker shines in cloudy skies.
Old ways crumble, new paths unfold,
In every trial, a heart of gold.

From depths of pain, strength is born,
A vibrant spirit, forever sworn.
Burning brightly, embers gleam,
The phoenix wakes from every dream.

Facing storms, I stand with pride,
In adversity, there's nothing to hide.
Every scar tells a story grand,
In my heart, I understand.

A blazing future, I will embrace,
Unbounded love, a warm embrace.
With wings outstretched, I take my flight,
The phoenix rising, bold and bright.

The Mirror Reflects a New Dawn

In morning light, I see my face,
A canvas clean, a fresh embrace.
Shadows fade, the past's undone,
A journey starts, the day begun.

With every glance, a chance to grow,
A whisper soft, the winds of flow.
In the reflection, hope resides,
An endless sea where love abides.

The dawn unfolds, a story to tell,
Each spark of change, a ringing bell.
With open heart, I seek the way,
A brighter realm, a brand new day.

Rebirth of an Untamed Spirit

From ashes high, the phoenix flies,
With fiery grace, it claims the skies.
Unbridled will, a heart that roars,
In every nerve, the spirit soars.

Through tangled woods, I roam and run,
A wild dance beneath the sun.
Every leap, a break from fear,
In freedom's breath, my truth is clear.

Unfettered dreams, like rivers wide,
The spark ignites, I cannot hide.
With every step, I rewrite fate,
An untamed soul, no need for wait.

Stripped Bare, I Flourish

Peeling layers, raw and real,
Beneath it all, I start to heal.
With every scar, a tale to share,
In vulnerability, I dare.

The world may see a fragile guise,
But strength exists beneath the lies.
In honest soil, my roots run deep,
From strife I rise, no need for sleep.

I blossom forth, in sun and rain,
A vibrant hue from all the pain.
Stripped of masks, I stand aware,
In naked truth, my spirit's fare.

Navigating the Labyrinth of Self

In twisted paths, I roam alone,
A puzzle lost, a heart of stone.
With every turn, I seek the core,
The echoes call, I yearn for more.

Mirrors twist, reflections fade,
Each step a dance, I am remade.
With candlelight, I search the dark,
A flicker bright ignites the spark.

Through shadows vast, I find my way,
The maze reveals, at break of day.
To know myself is not in vain,
In labyrinthine grace, I gain.

Illuminating My Hidden Corners

In shadows deep where secrets dwell,
I seek the light, my heart's farewell.
With every thought, I spark a flame,
Illuminating corners, shedding blame.

The whispers of the past do fade,
As courage blooms, my soul displayed.
With every step, I claim my space,
Revealing truth in every trace.

A gentle breath, I start to see,
The brighter path that's meant for me.
Unraveled threads of doubt unwind,
My spirit soars, my heart aligned.

In every crevice, light shall flow,
Transforming dark with vibrant glow.
In hidden corners, strength will rise,
Reflecting dreams beneath the skies.

A Canvas of Forgotten Dreams

A canvas bare, untouched by time,
Holds colors bold, yet lost in rhyme.
Forgotten hopes, in silence cry,
Awakening hearts that long to fly.

Each stroke of paint, a memory stirs,
A vision clear, as passion purrs.
With tender hands, I bring to life,
The dreams once lost, amidst the strife.

The palette spreads, like dawn's embrace,
Igniting spark in every space.
Resplendent hues of joy and pain,
A tapestry of love's refrain.

In every blend, a story told,
The dreams reborn, the heart consoled.
A canvas bright, my soul's decree,
Embracing all that's yet to be.

Shattering the Chains of Expectation

In silent chains, I once was bound,
With heavy hearts, I wore the crown.
The weight of others pressed me low,
As paths untraveled began to glow.

With every breath, I rise anew,
A fierce resolve, my spirit true.
The whispers fade, I claim my right,
To forge my path, to seek the light.

I shatter walls that held me tight,
Embracing freedom, taking flight.
The echo of my dreams resound,
In every heartbeat, courage found.

No longer molded by their hands,
I dance to rhythms life commands.
With every step, I break away,
Transforming night into bright day.

Rebuilding from Within

When pieces fall, like autumn's leaves,
I gather strength, my heart believes.
From shattered dreams, a spark ignites,
Rebuilding hope on starry nights.

Each crack a story, wisdom gained,
Through trials faced, and lessons trained.
With hands of grace, I mend the seams,
Creating worlds from quiet dreams.

The foundations laid, with love and care,
A shelter built, from thoughts laid bare.
Renewed by fire of inner might,
Emerging strong, I find my light.

In sacred space, I claim my voice,
Reinforcing faith, embracing choice.
From rubble rise, the soul anew,
Rebuilding life, my spirit true.

The Awakening of My Spirit

In silence, I hear the call,
A whispering breeze in the hall.
The shadows retreat from my heart,
A new journey is set to start.

I rise with the dawn's golden light,
Embracing the warmth, taking flight.
Each step forward, I begin to see,
The light within, so wild and free.

With every breath, I feel alive,
The spirit within begins to thrive.
Old chains of doubt fall away,
In this moment, I choose to stay.

Nature sings in harmonious grace,
Inviting me to join the race.
Together, we dance the sacred dance,
Awakening life in a fleeting glance.

Finally, I stand here whole,
Embracing life, body, and soul.
The awakening softly persists,
In every heartbeat, love exists.

Wings of Self-Love

In the mirror, I find my gaze,
A journey begun in gentle ways.
With every flaw, I learn to see,
The beauty alive deep within me.

My heart takes flight, unchained and wild,
Embracing the essence of this child.
The world unfolds with colors bright,
Each moment a canvas, pure delight.

Soft whispers of kindness, I share,
Nurturing love everywhere.
With every breath, I rise and grow,
Discovering depths I long to know.

Wings constructed from tender care,
Lift me high into the air.
With confidence, I break each mold,
In my heart, a story unfolds.

I am enough, I hear the song,
A melody gentle, clear, and strong.
With wings of love, I soar so high,
Embracing the truth, no need to lie.

Seeds of Change Beneath the Earth

In darkness, seeds begin their quest,
To awaken and grow, they must rest.
The earth cradles them in gentle care,
Whispers of change dance through the air.

Each moment, they drink from the night,
Nurtured by dreams, they draw in light.
Tiny sprouts push through the clay,
Emerging strong in a bright array.

Roots dig deeper, seeking the past,
Memories formed, shadows cast.
But with each drop of rain they find,
New life blossoms, unconfined.

Above the ground, they stretch and bloom,
Embracing life, dispelling gloom.
The cycle begins anew each day,
Transforming the night into a ballet.

Seeds of change, they rise and sway,
Reminders of hope in disarray.
Embodying strength in every breath,
The beauty of life, the dance with death.

Reflections in a Broken Mirror

Fragments scattered on the floor,
Each piece a tale, an open door.
A mosaic of light and dark,
Reflections whisper, ignite the spark.

In cracks and shatters, I see my face,
A thousand stories, each a trace.
The beauty lies in what is whole,
In every piece, a fractured soul.

Time weaves patterns, a delicate thread,
Connecting moments, the words unsaid.
In echoes of laughter, I hear the pain,
But even in storms, there's beauty gained.

I gather the pieces, one by one,
Turning the darkness into sun.
In every reflection, I learn to find,
A path of acceptance, gracefully kind.

So I embrace the mirror, cracked and true,
A testament to all that I've been through.
For in the broken, there's always a way,
To shine brighter with each passing day.

Rising from the Ashes

In shadows deep, I find my spark,
From the ruins, I'll leave my mark.
With every flame, I rise anew,
A phoenix born, my strength rings true.

The ashes call, they sing my name,
In the silence, I feel no shame.
A journey paved with pain and grace,
I'll take the leap, I'll find my place.

With wings spread wide, I chase the sky,
The past behind, I'm free to fly.
Each breath I take, a battle won,
My heart ignites, I am reborn.

In vibrant hues, the future glows,
Through every trial, my spirit grows.
From every tear, a river wide,
I'll carve my path, I'll turn the tide.

For in the dark, I've found my light,
The stars above, they guide my flight.
With hope as fuel, I'll burn so bright,
Rising now, I claim my right.

Embracing the Fragments

In shattered pieces, I find my way,
Each broken shard, a new display.
A tapestry of loss and gain,
In every crack, there blooms my pain.

I gather dreams like scattered leaves,
In whispered winds, my heart believes.
With open arms, I hold what's real,
The fragments speak, they help me heal.

Through tangled threads, my story spins,
In messy hues, my hope begins.
A quilt of strength, I proudly wear,
Each patch a tale, a reason to care.

The scars I bear, a badge of grace,
In every crack, I find my place.
With gentle hands, I mold my fate,
Embracing all, I learn, create.

In silence deep, I hear the song,
Of every piece, where I belong.
Together whole, in beauty's light,
From fragments forged, I rise in flight.

Sheet Music of My Heart

In quiet notes, my story flows,
With every beat, my spirit knows.
A melody, soft and sweet,
Each harmony, my heart's heartbeat.

The verses dance, a rhythmic sway,
In chords of love, I find my way.
With every pause, a breath I take,
In music's arms, my soul awakes.

The laughter rings, a joyful tune,
In twilight's glow, beneath the moon.
A symphony of hopes and dreams,
In gentle waves, my heart redeems.

The echoes linger, memories dear,
In every note, you'll find me here.
With passion bright, I weave the part,
This grand composition of my heart.

So let the music play the night,
In every sound, I find my light.
With open ears, I'll hear the call,
The sheet music, embracing all.

Whispers of a New Dawn

In twilight's hush, the world awakes,
A gentle breeze, the moment breaks.
The sun peeks out, a golden ray,
It brushes night away, gives way.

With colors bright, the sky transforms,
A canvas fresh, where hope conforms.
Each whisper soft, a promise made,
As shadows fade, the fears cascade.

The morning hum, a sweet embrace,
New beginnings in every space.
In fields of light, I'll wander free,
To dreams fulfilled, my heart's decree.

With every step, I shed the past,
A journey wide, my heart beats fast.
The whispers call, they guide my way,
Into the dawn of a brand new day.

For in this light, I see the truth,
A vivid spark, the thrill of youth.
In every ray, I find my song,
Whispers of hope, where I belong.

Awakened by the Storm

The thunder calls me from my dreams,
Rain whispers secrets in my ears.
Nature's fury, wild and free,
Awakens hope amidst my fears.

Lightning flashes, bright and bold,
A dance of power in the night.
Each drop of rain, a story told,
Bringing darkness into light.

Trees sway gently to the tune,
Branches reach out, strong and true.
The tempest sings a vibrant rune,
As I find strength in all that's new.

In chaos, beauty comes alive,
A symphony of earth and sky.
From the storm, I learn to thrive,
As every wave urges me to fly.

Awakened now, I stand so tall,
Grounded deep by nature's grace.
The storm may roar, but I won't fall,
In its embrace, I find my place.

Breaking through the Fog

Morning breaks, the fog drifts slow,
Hidden paths begin to show.
Silent whispers fill the air,
Promises linger everywhere.

Shadows dance where sunlight weaves,
Mysteries are wrapped in leaves.
Clearing thoughts come softly near,
As the horizon starts to clear.

Step by step, the world awakes,
In the light, the heart remakes.
Clarity shines on every face,
Finding courage in this space.

Fog retreats, the dawn unfolds,
Truth emerges, bright and bold.
In the glow, my spirit flies,
Touching dreams that fill the skies.

Breaking free, I take my stand,
With each moment, I understand.
The fog may come, but so does light,
In the dance of day and night.

A Dance with My Shadows

In the quiet of the night,
Shadows creep, avoiding light.
They beckon me to join the fray,
In a world where fears hold sway.

We twirl beneath the silver moon,
A haunting, melancholic tune.
Embraced by darkness, I find peace,
As whispers in the night increase.

Every step, a story shared,
The burdens borne, I have dared.
In their depths, I learn to see,
The hidden parts that set me free.

Through the dance, my heart takes flight,
Confronting fears that shun the light.
In the waltz of dusk and dawn,
I find the strength to carry on.

In my shadows, I find grace,
Each movement shapes a sacred space.
For in the dark, there's light to claim,
A dance with shadows, free from shame.

The Path From Silence to Sound

In the hush before the dawn,
A melody begins to spawn.
Quiet whispers call my name,
In stillness, I feel the flame.

Footsteps echo on the ground,
Every heartbeat makes a sound.
From silence blooms the song of day,
Pulsing rhythms lead the way.

Voices rise, a chorus bold,
In every note, a story told.
As shadows fade, the light expands,
Connecting dreams with open hands.

Harmony in every breath,
Life sings through the dance of death.
From quiet depths, a symphony,
Emerges bright, alive in me.

The path unfolds, as sounds collide,
In every heartbeat, I confide.
From silence grows a rich surround,
A journey shared, a world profound.

Breaking the Chains of Self-Doubt

In shadows deep, I often tread,
Where whispers creep, and courage fled.
Yet in the stillness, hope ignites,
And slowly shifts the darkest nights.

With every tear, a strength thus born,
A light within, where dreams are worn.
I rise amidst the fallen doubt,
Embracing all that life's about.

These chains that bind shall one day break,
For in my heart, there lies a quake.
A voice that roars despite the fear,
Each step I take draws me near.

In mirrors cracked, I see my fight,
Reflections forged from endless night.
Each scar a tale of battles won,
An anthem loud, my heart's begun.

So here I stand, no longer lost,
Awakened soul, I count the cost.
For breaking chains means I am free,
To claim my truth, my destiny.

Finding My Forgotten Song

In quiet corners of my mind,
A melody I thought resigned.
It whispers soft, a distant tune,
Beneath the sun, beneath the moon.

I seek the notes once lost in time,
Each rhythm stirs my heart to climb.
With tender hands, I search and play,
To find the song that slipped away.

Through golden fields, in laughter's grace,
I wander wide, I quicken pace.
Each echo calls, a siren's plea,
To sing the truth that sets me free.

So softly now, the chords return,
With every beat, my spirit yearns.
A harmony of life's embrace,
In every note, find my own place.

And when the final notes are sung,
I'll hold the song, forever young.
For every heart can find its tune,
And dance again beneath the moon.

Pages of a New Chapter

In winter's chill, I shed the past,
Embracing change, horizons vast.
Each page I turn, a story penned,
A brighter tale, unique to blend.

With ink of hope, I write anew,
A journey sparked with every hue.
The lines await—where shall I tread?
With open heart, I forge ahead.

Through valleys deep and mountains high,
I'll chase the stars across the sky.
With every word, my spirit grows,
In tales of dreams, the courage flows.

As seasons shift, my heart will soar,
Exploring realms I can't ignore.
In pen's embrace, the future gleams,
I grasp the power of my dreams.

So here I stand, the ink now dry,
With bold resolve, I'll reach the sky.
For every chapter holds a spark,
In pages blank, I'll leave my mark.

The Canvas of My Soul

Upon the canvas, colors blend,
In strokes of life, where shadows mend.
Each hue a whisper from my heart,
A timeless dance, a work of art.

With brush in hand, I paint the light,
In every line, find depth and height.
The swirls of joy, the lines of pain,
My soul's true essence, free and plain.

In vibrant reds, my passions blaze,
While blues hold tales of softer days.
Through greens of growth, I rise anew,
Embracing all that I pursue.

Every splash, a story told,
In shades of love, both warm and bold.
With every stroke, my spirit's free,
On this grand canvas, I will be.

So let the world behold my art,
A vibrant echo of my heart.
For in this space, I am whole,
Forever inked, the canvas of my soul.

Resilience in Fragile Moments

In shadows cast, we find our light,
Through storms that rage, we hold on tight.
With every fall, we rise anew,
Our spirits strong, we push on through.

Like flowers bloom in winter's grasp,
We find our strength, we hold, we clasp.
Each tear a seed, each wound a grace,
We face the world, we find our place.

The cracks reveal our inner fire,
A heart that beats, a soul inspired.
In fragile moments, courage grows,
Through darkest nights, our brilliance shows.

When hope seems lost, we forge ahead,
On fragile wings, we dare to tread.
For in our hearts, resilience lies,
In every fall, we learn to rise.

So let the winds of change be bold,
In every story, strength unfolds.
Our fragile moments, rich and deep,
In whispered dreams, our promise keep.

The Return of My Essence

From distant shores, I call my name,
Through waves of doubt, I fan the flame.
The winds of time, they twist and bend,
But in my heart, I find a friend.

In silent moments, I reclaim,
The threads of joy, my inner flame.
With every step, my truth I chart,
The journey calls, it sings my heart.

In shadows cast, my essence gleams,
Awakening from whispered dreams.
The past, a guide along the way,
In colors bright, I choose to stay.

The pieces lost, now intertwine,
In every breath, my spirit shines.
Returning home, I find my peace,
In every moment, sweet release.

So here I stand, a soul reborn,
In morning light, I greet the dawn.
The return of self, a sacred quest,
In every heartbeat, I find rest.

Sculpting My True Identity

With hands of dreams, I shape my soul,
In every curve, I find my whole.
The clay of life, it feels so bright,
In shadows cast, I mold my light.

Chipping away at doubt's embrace,
I carve a path, I find my place.
Each layer stripped reveals my core,
In gentle strokes, I long for more.

Through trials fierce, my spirit bends,
Yet like the river, it never ends.
In sculptor's hands, my heart is free,
Creating art, my destiny.

The echoes of my past still sing,
In every note, my essence clings.
With tools of grace and love bestowed,
I shape my being, truth bestowed.

So here I stand, a work in view,
In every shade, my colors true.
Sculpting self, with every breath,
My masterpiece, beyond all depth.

Glimmers of Lost Dreams

In twilight's glow, we search for beams,
Flickers bright of lost, sweet dreams.
Through tangled paths, our hearts still soar,
In whispered hopes, we yearn for more.

The shadows linger, but stars ignite,
Even in darkness, we find the light.
Each memory, a shining thread,
In fabric woven, dreams we spread.

The echoes of what once might be,
Dance in the night, wild and free.
In every failure, glimmers gleam,
A tapestry of hope's soft dream.

Let not the past define our flight,
For in each ending, we find our light.
Through every scar, our story speaks,
In every silence, strength it seeks.

So gather 'round, the spark remains,
In every heart, lost dream sustains.
With open arms, we greet the morn,
In glimmers bright, new dreams are born.

Symphony of Self-Acceptance

In shadows deep, I find my song,
Each note a truth where I belong.
The flaws I wear become my grace,
A symphony in this quiet space.

I dance with fears that once held tight,
Embrace the dark, and claim the light.
Each whisper soft, my heart reveals,
The beauty found in how it feels.

With every beat, I learn to rise,
To meet my dreams beyond the skies.
Imperfections, a canvas raw,
A masterpiece I now adore.

In harmony, I shed my doubt,
A melody that sings about,
The journey inward, brave and true,
In self-acceptance, I renew.

The past a tune that fades away,
I choose the path, come what may.
With open heart, I greet the dawn,
In my own symphony, I'm reborn.

Unraveled Threads and New Beginnings

In tangled knots of yesterday,
I find the strength to break away.
Each thread unwinds with gentle grace,
A new path shows, a brighter place.

The woven past is rich and bold,
Yet silver linings start to unfold.
In every tear, a lesson learned,
From ashes deep, my spirit burned.

With hands now free, I spin anew,
A tapestry of dreams in view.
Each color bright, each pattern fine,
Unraveled threads, my life divine.

I gather hope, a vibrant hue,
In every stitch, my truth shines through.
A future bright with endless range,
In every heartbeats' subtle change.

The journey's long, the path is wide,
With faith, I take each hopeful stride.
Unraveled threads, my heart takes flight,
Embracing all, I greet the light.

The Map of My Inner Landscape

In the valleys of my silent mind,
A world unfolds, unique and kind.
Mountains rise, with peaks of doubt,
Yet rivers flow, and lights break out.

Each step I take, a path revealed,
Through hidden thoughts, my heart is healed.
The flora blooms where courage grows,
A vibrant land where wildness flows.

In secret caves, my fears reside,
Yet in their shadows, hope won't hide.
I map my journeys, twist and turn,
With every page, new lessons learned.

The compass points to who I am,
Guided by a gentle hand.
Through storms that rage and skies so blue,
My inner landscape calls me true.

With every breath, I forge ahead,
Past trails of doubt, where angels tread.
In this vast world, I find my peace,
A map of dreams, my soul's release.

Unmasking the True Essence

Beneath the masks, my spirit hides,
In layers thick, my heart abides.
With each façade, I play my role,
Yet long for truth to heal my soul.

The smiles I wear, a clever guise,
Conceal the storms behind my eyes.
But in the quiet, whispers call,
To peel the layers, break the wall.

I shed the weight of other's views,
Embrace the light in honest hues.
With courage found in every tear,
I step into the space I steer.

Each breath a bridge to who I am,
A heart laid bare, no need to scam.
In raw vulnerability, I stand,
Unmasking truth with open hands.

The essence shines, a radiant glow,
In self-discovery, I come to know.
There's beauty found in simply me,
Unmasked, unchained, I am set free.

Steps Toward My Own Horizon

With each step I take, I find my ground,
New paths unfolding all around.
The sun is rising, casting light,
Guiding me through the morning bright.

Dreams whisper softly in the breeze,
Encouraging me to move with ease.
Mountains loom, daunting and tall,
But I won't stumble, I won't fall.

The sky ahead, a canvas wide,
I paint my hopes, my heart, my pride.
Each breath I take, a moment seized,
In this journey, my soul is pleased.

Ahead of me, the horizon calls,
With open arms, it breaks my walls.
A leap of faith, a daring flight,
Into the day, ignited light.

So here I stand, heart open wide,
Embracing change, a joyful ride.
With every step, I leave behind,
The shackles of doubt that once confined.

The Sound of My Own Laughter

Echoes of joy dance in the air,
A melody sweet, beyond compare.
With every chuckle, burdens fade,
Living in bliss, I am unafraid.

Like raindrops falling on thirsty ground,
My laughter spills, a joyous sound.
It carries me high, on wings of glee,
In the lightness, I find the key.

Moments shared, in playful jest,
Remind me that I'm truly blessed.
In the company of friends so dear,
Our laughter lingers, clear and near.

I dance with shadows, embrace the light,
Each giggle born from pure delight.
In the chorus of life, I play my part,
Sowing seeds of joy, heart to heart.

So let the laughter be my guide,
In every moment, I take in stride.
With open arms and a heart so free,
The sound of my laughter, a symphony.

Embracing the joy of who I am,
A radiant flame, fiercely I stand.
In laughter's embrace, my spirit soars,
Unlocking dreams behind closed doors.

Embracing the Storm Within

Whispers within, a tempest brews,
Winds of change, I choose to fuse.
Dark clouds gather, but I won't flee,
In this storm, I yearn to be free.

Lightning strikes, illuminating doubt,
A dance of shadows, I scream and shout.
The rain may pour, but I will stand,
Embracing the chaos, heart in hand.

A thunderous roar awakens my soul,
Through fierce winds, I learn to be whole.
The torrent offers strength renewed,
In the tempest, I find my truth.

I've weathered struggles, I've felt the pain,
But through it all, I rise again.
Storms may batter, but I won't break,
In every challenge, new paths I make.

So let the winds howl, let the rain descend,
In the heart of the storm, I'm learning to mend.
With every drop, my spirit ignites,
In this wild dance, my heart takes flight.

A Symphony of Self-Affirmation

Notes of courage, softly sung,
In the choir of life, I am among.
With each refrain, I lift my voice,
In the symphony, I find my choice.

Melodies weave through heart and soul,
Embracing the parts that make me whole.
Every whisper, a gentle embrace,
In the music of me, I find my place.

Harmony soars, soaring high,
A testament that I can try.
I'll play my part, I'll take the stage,
In every note, I exit the cage.

With each crescendo, fears subside,
In this symphony, I take pride.
Resonating truth, in vibrant hues,
I celebrate me, all that I choose.

The music plays on, a sacred dance,
In every beat, I find my chance.
So here I stand, strong and free,
In this symphony of self, I'll be me.

The Phoenix Within

In ashes deep, a spark remains,
From darkest night, the fire gains.
Wings unfurl beneath the glow,
Rebirth beckons, life will flow.

From every fall, a lesson learned,
Through trials faced, the spirit burned.
With strength anew, I rise and soar,
The phoenix lives, forevermore.

Through flames that dance, I find my way,
Transforming fears into the day.
The past may sting, but I won't fall,
A brighter tomorrow answers the call.

Embrace the heat, embrace the light,
In shadows' grip, I find my might.
With every tear, a moment grows,
Awakening strength, the phoenix glows.

Secrets of My Heart's Journey

In whispers soft, my secrets hide,
Journeying deep, where dreams abide.
Through valleys low, and mountains high,
I seek the truth, beneath the sky.

Each heartbeat tells a tale untold,
In silent nights, my thoughts unfold.
Paths entwined, in shadows cast,
A tapestry of future and past.

With every step, I learn to trust,
In moments bright and in the dust.
With hope as guide, I chart the course,
A tapestry stitched with love's own force.

In every tear, a glimmer shines,
Through darkness deep, my spirit climbs.
The journey lives, a sacred art,
My truth revealed, the song of heart.

Bridging the Past and Future

Across the river, time does flow,
Connecting where the wild winds blow.
With memories held, and dreams to weave,
I stand on shores, where none deceive.

The echoes of a lifetime past,
Guide my steps, their shadows cast.
With every bridge, I choose to cross,
Transforming pain, reclaiming loss.

The future whispers, bright and near,
A promise made, to face my fear.
In twilight's glow, the dawn will break,
A journey shared, for love's own sake.

With open heart, I greet the day,
For each new dawn, a brighter way.
In harmony, the past and now,
I forge ahead, with strength I vow.

A New Dawn Rising

With sunlit skies, the day begins,
A canvas fresh, where hope soon spins.
The shadows fade, the light awakes,
A promise bright, the world remakes.

Each ray of gold, a chance to shine,
In every heart, a life divine.
The journey's path unfurls anew,
With dreams refreshed, the spirit true.

With every moment, nature's grace,
A new dawn rises, time to embrace.
The past may linger, but I let go,
With open arms, I greet the flow.

Let courage guide, let love ignite,
With every breath, I chase the light.
The world awaits, so vast and wide,
In this new dawn, I take my stride.

Ascending into My Own Power

With every step, I rise anew,
Unfolding strength I never knew.
Roots entwined in earth so deep,
Awakening dreams, no more to sleep.

Wings unfurl, I touch the sky,
Embracing fears, I learn to fly.
The light within begins to bloom,
Casting shadows from the room.

Battles fought, I've gained my ground,
In silence, my voice, it's found.
Breaking chains that held me fast,
My spirit shines, free at last.

Mountains high, I stand up tall,
Echoes whisper through the hall.
In this power, I see my way,
Guided by the light of day.

A journey forged with heart and mind,
In every challenge, strength I find.
Ascending now, I take my stand,
In my own power, life expands.

Awakening the Undiscovered

In the stillness, dreams arise,
Hidden paths beneath the skies.
Glimmers spark in shadowed space,
Where I seek my rightful place.

Voices call from deep within,
Stirring hopes that once had been.
Whispers of a life untold,
In the brave, the meek, the bold.

Curiosity ignites the fire,
Reaching out, I dare aspire.
Through the mist, I find the light,
Illuminating all my might.

Every heartbeat feels the change,
Life's rhythm, wild and strange.
Awakening the undiscovered,
In this moment, I'm uncovered.

With each thought that takes its flight,
I embrace the dance of light.
Journey's start, I'll claim my role,
Awakening my very soul.

From Shadows to Radiance

In shadows deep, I once was bound,
A silent cry, a muffled sound.
Yet deep inside, a spark still glowed,
Unseen paths awaited, bestowed.

I gathered courage, took a stand,
To break the chains and leave the sand.
With every tear, the darkness fades,
Illuminated, new light invades.

The dawn emerges, fresh and bright,
Chasing away the long, dark night.
From shadows thick to radiance clear,
I rise, I shine, I persevere.

Each moment lived, a chance to grow,
Bringing forth the inner glow.
From the depths, I find my way,
Transcending shadows, come what may.

With every heartbeat, I reclaim,
The strength within, I fan the flame.
From shadows vast to radiance true,
A journey bright, forever new.

Echoes of My Own Voice

In the quiet, I start to hear,
The echoes of my voice so clear.
Resonating through the night,
Filling spaces with their light.

A gentle sound that flows like streams,
Carrying my unspoken dreams.
In the chaos, profound and loud,
I find my truth, I stand unbowed.

Whispers linger, dance around,
In solitude, my strength is found.
Listening close, my heart aligns,
In echoes vast, my spirit shines.

Each note, a story yet untold,
In rhythms soft, I feel the bold.
From silence strong, I break the mold,
Echoes speak, my journey unfolds.

With every breath, my voice ascends,
A melody that never ends.
In echoes rich, I'm learning grace,
Finding power in my own space.

Echoes of My Own Heartbeat

In the silence, I can hear,
Soft whispers from deep within,
A rhythm that casts out fear,
Each pulse, a tale of where I've been.

Shadows dance in flickering light,
Chasing dreams as they take flight,
Every beat a step I find,
Mapping trails of heart and mind.

Resilient echoes fill the night,
Carrying fragments of my fight,
The melody, both soft and strong,
Guiding me where I belong.

In solitude, I face the dusk,
Embracing thoughts, a gentle must,
With every sigh, a truth laid bare,
In the stillness, I breathe my prayer.

Through valleys deep and mountains high,
Each heartbeat calls to me, a sigh,
Embodying all that I have sought,
Resonating, the lessons taught.

Breaking Free from the Mould

The chains that bind, I cast away,
Unfolding wings where skies are grey,
In every crack, the light peeks through,
A world renewed, where I break through.

No longer shaped by shadows past,
I rise above, my spirit cast,
In colors bright, I choose to shine,
A silhouette, distinctly mine.

With every step, a path I forge,
Awakening dreams that I can gorge,
The mould no longer holds me tight,
My essence blooms, a dazzling sight.

Unwritten lines, a tale untold,
In courage warm, I find the bold,
I dance anew, a fluid grace,
With love and hope, my heart's embrace.

The world expands, horizons vast,
Each moment seized, a spell is cast,
From silence spring, my voice shall soar,
In breaking free, I find my core.

The Colors of My True Self

In hues of life, my heart takes flight,
A canvas splashed with pure delight,
From crimson love to azure dreams,
Each stroke reflects my silent screams.

Beneath the layers, stories weave,
In patterns bold, I too believe,
Emerging vibrant, rich and raw,
Embracing all that I once saw.

The palette shifts with every mood,
Beneath the calm, a deeper brood,
In shades of gold, I find the glow,
Revealing colors only I know.

In twilight's brush, I find my peace,
A symphony of thoughts that cease,
Each pigment rich with tales to share,
Reflecting truths laid open, bare.

Through art, my spirit learns to tell,
In vivid strokes, I weave the spell,
The colors dance, a vibrant blend,
In every shade, I find my friend.

Pieces of Me Reassembled

Shattered dreams upon the floor,
Each fragment holds a timeless score,
In quiet moments, I collect,
The pieces that time can't neglect.

With gentle hands, I mold them close,
A puzzle formed, a timely dose,
Through lens of love, each shard I see,
In every break, a part of me.

From darkness springs a brighter light,
A tapestry from endless night,
With threads of gold, I weave the past,
Creating strength, a life repassed.

Resilience blooms in heart's embrace,
Each lesson learned, a sacred space,
In fragile forms, I find my grace,
A tapestry time can't erase.

The journey taken, wise and deep,
In every cut, a promise keeps,
With pieces joined, I stand anew,
A work of art, my spirit true.

Unfolding the Hand of Fate

In whispers soft, the stories weave,
Tales of dreams that we conceive.
A gentle tug, the threads align,
In fate's embrace, our stars combine.

Through twisted paths, we wander far,
Guided by the light of a distant star.
Each choice a step, each breath a chance,
In life's grand dance, we find romance.

With every turn, a lesson learned,
In shadows cast, our spirits burned.
A tapestry of joy and pain,
In every drop, a hint of rain.

The heart shall soar, the spirit thrive,
As long as hope keeps dreams alive.
In every fold, a mystery waits,
Unfolding gently, the hand of fate.

So take my hand, let's face the dawn,
Together brave, we journey on.
With every heartbeat, love's refrain,
In the grip of fate, we'll break our chain.

Uncharted Territory

Where the wild winds blow and waters churn,
In a world reborn, we yearn and learn.
No maps to guide, no paths to trace,
In uncharted lands, we seek our place.

The mountains rise, an ancient call,
Rivers rush, and shadows fall.
With every step, the unknown near,
In the heart's embrace, we conquer fear.

Across the plains, the echoes roam,
In the vast unknown, we make our home.
Trailblazers bold, in the night we run,
Under the gaze of the watchful sun.

The stars above, our compass bright,
A constellation of hope and light.
In untouched fields, we find our way,
Through uncharted dreams, we'll boldly sway.

So let us wander, hand in hand,
In the magic of this unspoiled land.
For in the wild, our spirits soar,
In uncharted territory, we'll explore.

A Heart Untethered

In restless skies, where eagles fly,
A heart untethered learns to sigh.
With every beat, it seeks to roam,
In search of love, it finds a home.

Through tangled woods, and rivers wide,
With open arms, the world as guide.
Each whisper soft, a promise made,
In dance of shadows, fears still fade.

The winds may call, the sea may churn,
In every loss, we find a turn.
A heart unbound, it sings aloud,
In melodies soft, under the clouds.

Through valleys deep, and mountains tall,
With courage strong, we rise, we fall.
Yet in each step, we find our grace,
A heart untethered finds its place.

So let it beat, let it feel free,
In every moment, just let it be.
For in this life, we wander far,
With a heart untethered, we'll reach each star.

In Search of My Own Horizon

Beyond the hills where sunlight gleams,
In search of truth, I chase my dreams.
With each new dawn, a canvas wide,
Incolorful splashes, the heart's true guide.

The waves may crash, the storms may roar,
Yet in the chaos, I'll seek for more.
With every rise and every fall,
I'll find my voice; I'll hear the call.

Through forests dense, and skies of grey,
In every shadow, I'll find my way.
With open eyes and willing heart,
In search of light, I won't depart.

The trails I blaze, the paths unknown,
In each new step, I'll find my throne.
For in the journey, truth will lie,
In search of my own horizon, I fly.

So take a breath, embrace the ride,
With every heartbeat, keep your stride.
For in this quest, I'll rise and soar,
In search of a horizon, forever more.

Daring to Dance in My Own Light

Underneath the starry sky,
I twirl with dreams untold.
Each step, a brave flight,
In my heart, a fire bold.

Whispers of doubt fade away,
As I move, I find my way.
With every beat of joy,
I reclaim what I enjoy.

Guided by the moon's embrace,
I feel my spirit race.
No longer held by fear,
In this moment, I am here.

Around me, shadows sway,
Yet my light holds them at bay.
With laughter as my grace,
I dance in my chosen space.

Embracing the glow so bright,
I dare to dance through the night.
In freedom, I'll ignite,
An anthem of pure delight.

Whispered Truths of the Heart

In silence, it softly speaks,
A melody of gentle sighs.
Hidden in the quiet peaks,
The heart knows where it lies.

Secrets wrapped in soft embrace,
Yearning to find the light.
With each pulse, a warm trace,
Guiding dreams into flight.

Gentle winds carry the sound,
A rustling through the trees.
The truths that seek to be found,
Rising like morning breeze.

In shadows, it finds its way,
Illuminating the dark.
A whisper on the day,
Awakening the spark.

Listen closely, take your time,
For love's message is clear.
In every note, a rhyme,
Drawing the heart near.

Anchored in My Own Story

Beneath the waves, I stand tall,
My roots run deep in the ground.
With every rise and every fall,
In my truth, I am found.

Pages turned, a tale unfolds,
Of courage in the night.
Each chapter, a treasure told,
In shadows, I find light.

Memories woven like threads,
Embracing the moments dear.
In every word, a journey spreads,
Filling my heart with cheer.

Anchored firm in my design,
I'll sail through storms and strife.
With every breath, I align,
Living my fullest life.

The anchor of my soul shines bright,
In the depths, where I belong.
With every star, I take flight,
In my heart, an endless song.

Reclaiming the Power of Silence

In stillness, whispers grow loud,
In quiet, my spirit wakes.
Lost in a bustling crowd,
I find peace in the breaks.

Each breath, a soothing balm,
A moment to reflect.
In silence, I feel calm,
A world in me to detect.

Thoughts dance like leaves in air,
Unraveled and set free.
In solitude, a prayer,
Connecting deeply with me.

Language of the heart unfolds,
In the hush where I reside.
Emerging from stories old,
In silence, I confide.

Reclaiming power once lost,
With each pause, I grow wise.
The beauty comes at a cost,
In silence, I rise.

Awakening the Echoes

In the quiet dawn, whispers call,
Voices of shadows, memories small.
Gentle breezes stir the past,
Echoes of laughter, they hold fast.

With every step, the world awakes,
Resonant chords, the silence shakes.
Heartbeats thrum to a rhythmic beat,
Awakening life beneath our feet.

In the stillness, the spirit sings,
Carrying hope on delicate wings.
A tapestry woven with threads of time,
Each echo a note, a sacred rhyme.

Eyes open wide to the shining hues,
Painting horizons with vibrant views.
The dawn of self, a radiant glow,
Awakening echoes of long ago.

Through fields of dreams, we boldly tread,
Following whispers, where we are led.
The past and present unite as one,
Awakening echoes, our journey begun.

Finding My Lost Voice

In the depths of silence, I once lay,
A muted heart, words lost in fray.
Searching for clarity in the night,
Yearning to speak, to find my light.

The mirror reflects a face unknown,
A shadowed figure, feeling alone.
With every breath, courage ignites,
To reclaim the song within those nights.

Softly, the whispers begin to rise,
A chorus of strength and gentle cries.
Each note a promise, a step to take,
Finding my voice, for my own sake.

Through valleys of doubt, I wander wide,
Discovering rhythms I cannot hide.
With every echo, I gather my truth,
In the melody, I rediscover youth.

Boldly I sing, the past in my song,
For in this journey, I truly belong.
Finding my voice, I soar above,
In every note, I feel the love.

Threads of Self Rediscovered

In the fabric of life, threads intertwine,
Each moment, a stitch, a design so fine.
Woven with care, stories unfold,
A tapestry rich, vibrant and bold.

Through shadows and light, I search the seams,
Unraveling dreams, exploring my schemes.
Every thread whispers, tales of old,
Connecting the past with futures untold.

Knot by knot, I pull and I weave,
Embracing the truths, ready to grieve.
For in the unraveling, I find my place,
Threads of self, a delicate grace.

The colors of courage, joy, and sorrow,
Intertwined with hope for tomorrow.
Each strand a journey, a wild embrace,
Threads of self lead me to grace.

I hand-stitch my legacy, firm and true,
Creating a story that's vibrant and new.
With each woven layer, I discover me,
Threads of self, setting my spirit free.

Unfolding the True Essence

In the stillness, I sense the glow,
Layers of self, ready to show.
Petals unfurl in the morning light,
Unfolding truths, taking flight.

With gentle hands, the past I tend,
Nurturing seeds that twist and bend.
The garden of spirit begins to bloom,
A fragrant dance dispelling the gloom.

Each moment a blossom, bursting with grace,
Inviting the world to witness my space.
In the heart of silence, I hear the call,
Unfolding essence, I stand tall.

The journey of self, a path so wide,
With every step, I walk in pride.
Embracing the shadows, the light breaks through,
Unfolding the essence of all that is true.

As I shed my layers, I rise anew,
With every heartbeat, I find my due.
In the tapestry of life, I see the thread,
Unfolding the essence, where dreams are led.

Lifting the Veil of Uncertainty

In shadows deep, where doubts reside,
A flicker shines, the heart's true guide.
With every breath, the clouds do part,
   Revealing light within the heart.

Fear whispers low, yet courage calls,
   To rise above the silent walls.
With open eyes, the world is cleared,
Embracing truths once held in fear.

The path ahead may twist and turn,
   But in its lessons, we shall learn.
Each step we take, with faith anew,
Unveiling dreams that once we knew.

In twilight's glow, hope softly glows,
   A seed of joy, the spirit sows.
With every leap, we brave the night,
   Finding strength in inner light.

So lift the veil, release the bind,
In every shadow, love you'll find.
Embrace the journey, hearts can heal,
   Together we'll lift the veil of zeal.

Whispers of My Soul's Truth

In silent depths, my heart does sing,
A melody of everything.
With gentle whispers, truths unfold,
A tapestry of dreams retold.

Beneath the chaos, stillness reigns,
Absorbing joys and humble pains.
Each note a brush, each breath a stroke,
In realms of light, my spirit woke.

The echoes chase the fleeting fear,
In quiet moments, I draw near.
To listen close, the soul's sweet rhyme,
A dance of essence, born of time.

With every heartbeat, wisdom flows,
Through cracks of doubt, the beauty grows.
In darkness deep, I find my voice,
Awakening my truest choice.

So let me wander, let me roam,
In whispers soft, I'll find my home.
With courage bright, I stand awake,
My soul's truth sings for love's own sake.

Threads of Destiny Rewoven

In every thread, a story spun,
From silent hopes to battles won.
Each twist and turn, a sacred bind,
Unfolding paths of heart and mind.

Time weaves patterns, bright and bold,
Through endless dreams and tales retold.
With every stitch, our futures align,
Creating tapestries, pure and divine.

In shadows cast, we find the light,
Resilient spirits take to flight.
With patient hands, the loom we guide,
As destiny flows like a gentle tide.

Embrace the change, let go of fears,
The threads reveal what each heart hears.
Together danced in cosmic play,
Rewoven threads seize the day.

So gather close, take heed of fate,
In woven dreams we'll contemplate.
For every thread, a chance to grow,
Creating worlds in every flow.

Planting Seeds of Self-Belief

In fertile ground, the seeds are sown,
With whispers soft, they've gently grown.
A sprout of courage breaks the earth,
To find the light, embrace its worth.

With tending hands, we nurture dreams,
In quiet faith, the spirit gleams.
Through storms that shake and sun that warms,
The roots dig deep, through all life's storms.

Each doubt a shadow, brushed away,
As blossoms rise to greet the day.
With every care, the heart takes flight,
In blooms of hope, we find our light.

So plant your dreams, let them take root,
In fields of heart, the soul will shoot.
With trust in self, the truth revealed,
Each seed of faith becomes our shield.

Through trials faced, the garden grows,
In vibrant hues, the spirit flows.
With every harvest, love receives,
The bounty born from self-beliefs.

Charting My Own Course

With compass in hand, I sail the seas,
Wind in my sails, I move with ease.
No map to follow, just stars above,
Guided by dreams and the strength of love.

Through storms I wander, undaunted and free,
Each wave a challenge, a part of me.
The horizon glows, a promise untold,
In the journey ahead, my spirit grows bold.

With each passing day, I learn and explore,
The world my canvas, my heart the core.
Adventure awaits on this path I tread,
New stories unfold as I move ahead.

The tide pulls my heart, it takes me away,
Into the unknown, come what may.
With courage to steer through dusk and dawn,
I chart my course, for new dreams are born.

In silence I find the strength to believe,
In the choices I make, I truly achieve.
Each step that I take, a mark of my might,
In the vastness of life, I embrace the light.

Blossoming Beyond the Shadows

In the hush of night, a whisper blooms,
Petals unfold, dispelling the glooms.
Colors awaken, vibrant and bright,
As dreams take wing, embraced by the light.

From cracks in the stone, resilience will rise,
Reaching for warmth under expansive skies.
Each struggle I face, a lesson to know,
In the garden of life, I learn how to grow.

Through seasons of change, I dance with the breeze,
Finding my strength in the depths of the trees.
In shadows I've lingered, but now I will soar,
With roots ever firm, I open the door.

Transformation unfolds, a story anew,
Embracing the rain as it nourishes, too.
I blossom in beauty, fierce and unbowed,
Reveling boldly, no fear of the crowd.

In full bloom, I stand, a beacon so bright,
Beyond all the shadows, I chase my own light.
With petals uncurled, my spirit renewed,
In the garden of dreams, my soul is imbued.

The Art of Rediscovery

In the quiet spaces, I search for the lost,
Memories woven with love, at a cost.
Fragments of laughter, a bittersweet song,
In the heart's hidden corners, where I belong.

Journeying inward, through time's gentle flow,
Rediscovering stories that once made me glow.
Each page turned softly, reveals a lost part,
As I piece together the threads of my heart.

In moments of stillness, the truth starts to shine,
Rekindling the passions that once felt divine.
With brush strokes of hope, I paint my new tale,
An artist of life, through the storms I prevail.

The echoes of silence invite me to see,
The beauty in moments I thought would not be.
With every reflection, I find strength anew,
The art of rediscovery, profound and true.

In the tapestry woven with colors and grace,
I celebrate me in this tender embrace.
Each step on this journey, with wisdom, I guide,
In the mirror of time, I wear my pride.

Writing My Name in Bold Letters

With ink in my hand, I craft my own fate,
Each letter a step, I will not be late.
My story unfolds on this canvas of white,
With passion and fire, I embrace the light.

No longer in shadows where whispers reside,
I carve out my truths with unwavering pride.
In vibrant strokes, my dreams come alive,
Writing my name, where my spirit will thrive.

The pen is my sword, my shield, and my voice,
Through every challenge, I will make my choice.
With courage as ink, and hope as my guide,
I strive for the mountains, where dreams coincide.

In chapters of struggle, resilience springs forth,
Each page a reminder of my inner worth.
Writing my name with a flourish so bold,
In the tale of my life, let my heart be told.

In the book of existence, my legacy flows,
With every new line, my true essence shows.
No fear of the judgment, I take a deep breath,
For writing my name is a dance with life, not death.

Symphony of Healing

In gentle whispers, hopes arise,
A tender heart begins to mend.
With every note, the spirit flies,
In time, the brokenness can end.

In shadows cast, there lies the light,
Harmony where pain once dwelled.
Each melody, a path to bright,
A song of strength, the heart upheld.

The rhythms deep, the pulse of grace,
A lullaby for weary souls.
In every tear, a sacred space,
As music weaves through life's great holes.

From silence comes a sweet refrain,
Awakening the dormant beat.
In chaos, beauty born of pain,
A symphony that feels complete.

So dance with me, embrace the sound,
Let healing wash our worries free.
Together, lost and then we're found,
In symphonies of jubilee.

A Quest for Inner Freedom

In shadowed corners of the mind,
The chains that bind, they start to fray.
With every step, a truth we find,
To seek the dawn, to find the way.

Unraveled thoughts begin to soar,
The heart, a compass brave and true.
With courage found, we crave for more,
In every choice, the self renews.

Through tangled paths and winding roads,
The spirit yearns for open skies.
Each burden shed, a weight unloads,
As we embrace our own true rise.

The journey countless souls have sought,
To break the mold and cast aside.
In every lesson, wisdom taught,
To claim the freedom that's inside.

So follow dreams and break the wall,
With fearless hearts, let courage lead.
In questing forth, we stand up tall,
In inner peace, our spirits freed.

The Colors of My Reawakening

From muted grays to vibrant hues,
A canvas stretched, my heart laid bare.
In every stroke, a spark, a muse,
The colors dance in morning air.

Emerging light, a warm embrace,
In yellow rays, I find my song.
The reds ignite a fierce new place,
In swirling hearts, where I belong.

Again I bloom, once lost, now found,
The petals bright, the scents of spring.
In every shade, my joys abound,
In nature's pulse, my spirit sings.

Each brush depicts a tale untold,
With blues that soothe and greens that heal.
The colors rich, the stories bold,
In vivid trails, my heart will feel.

Reawakening in vibrant cheer,
The palette shifts, a life reborn.
In each new day, I hold so dear,
In colors bright, I greet the dawn.

Echoes of the Past and Present

In whispered tales, the ages blend,
With every word, a truth to find.
The echoes call, from souls long spent,
As memories weave through space and time.

Old photographs, the laughter bright,
The sorrow carved within the years.
In shadows cast by fading light,
The past still breathes, it draws us near.

Through whispered winds, the voices sway,
A haunting song of might and grace.
In sunny fields where children play,
The present flows, a warm embrace.

The stories live within our veins,
Each heartbeat links the now and then.
In joy and loss, the wisdom reigns,
A tapestry both thick and thin.

So let us sing both loud and clear,
For every echo serves a role.
In past and present, we adhere,
Together, we become whole souls.

Navigating the Labyrinth Within

In shadows deep, I wander slow,
Through winding paths where thoughts do flow.
The heart's whispers guide my way,
In silence, I find what words can't say.

Each turn reveals a hidden truth,
Retreating time unveils my youth.
Fragments lost, yet still I seek,
The strength to face the voice that's weak.

Labyrinth of fears, I tread with care,
Each corner turned, a moment rare.
Illusions fade, as wisdom grows,
In every pulse, my spirit glows.

The map I draw is forged by pain,
Yet joy and love have much to gain.
With every step, my soul ignites,
A dance within, a spark that fights.

So here I stand, amidst the maze,
Embracing both the dark and blaze.
In inner depths, I'll find my way,
A journey long, yet rich in play.

A Tapestry of New Possibilities

Threads of color, bright and bold,
Woven tales of life unfold.
Each stitch a dream, a chance to weave,
A future bright, I dare believe.

The loom of fate keeps turning fast,
With every choice, new shadows cast.
A myriad paths that I can take,
In every moment, new dreams awake.

With needle poised, I craft my art,
A tapestry that sings from the heart.
The patterns shift, they twist, they flow,
In every thread, new visions glow.

From dark to light, the colors change,
In every hue, I feel the range.
Embracing all that life imparts,
Stitching together our myriad parts.

The tapestry grows, from small to grand,
A story woven by my hand.
In every knot, new hope ignites,
A future shaped by endless sights.

Serendipity of Self-Discovery

In quiet moments, soft and still,
Life reveals its gentle thrill.
A chance encounter, simple grace,
Awakens joy, a warm embrace.

Through winding paths of twist and turn,
Lessons come from what we learn.
In chaos found, a spark ignites,
Truth emerges in quiet nights.

With open heart and mind to roam,
I find the essence of my home.
Each serendipity leads me there,
To cherish moments, light as air.

The journey's rich, a treasure trove,
In spaces deep, my spirit roves.
Each layer peeled reveals the core,
Unraveling what I was before.

Through every chance and twist of fate,
I celebrate, I contemplate.
In self-discovery, I find my way,
A dance of joy in life's ballet.

Rewriting My Own Narrative

With pen in hand, I draft the scene,
New words will flow, my voice serene.
The past is ink, the future's bright,
In every line, I seek the light.

Each chapter's pain, a lesson learned,
From ashes, fires of strength are burned.
The story bends, yet stays my own,
In every struggle, seeds are sown.

Revising tales with courage's might,
Transforming shadows into light.
Old burdens shed, like autumn leaves,
Embracing hope that never grieves.

Words reform, a tapestry spun,
Where dreams collide, new journeys run.
With every page, I claim my name,
In ownership, I play the game.

So here I stand, the author bold,
Crafting futures yet untold.
In every stroke, my spirit thrives,
Rewriting life, where passion drives.

Dancing with My Own Shadow

In the twilight, I twirl and sway,
My shadow follows, a silent play.
Feet whisper softly upon the ground,
In the dance of dusk, I'm unbound.

A partner carved from light and dark,
Together we weave, leave our mark.
With every spin, I learn to trust,
In the rhythm of me, there's a spark.

Echoes laugh in the evening breeze,
As I surrender, my mind finds ease.
Each step a story, each turn a song,
In this delicate dance, I belong.

Through flickering flames of the near-off night,
I guide my shadow into the light.
In this embrace, we endlessly soar,
Two souls in motion, forevermore.

In the silence, we find our grace,
A timeless dance, a sacred space.
In every heartbeat, in every glance,
I dance with my shadow, and take the chance.

Embracing the Tapestry of Me

Threads of color weave and spin,
Each hue a truth that lies within.
In the fabric of life, I find my place,
A tapestry rich, a warm embrace.

Every stitch a tale, every patch a part,
Woven together, a work of art.
In the weave of my being, stories collide,
In this intricate pattern, I confide.

Gentle hands pull and tug with care,
Binding memories with love laid bare.
Each fraying edge, a lesson learned,
In the warmth of the weave, my heart's returned.

Emotions spill like colors bright,
Filling the void with pure delight.
Through joy and sorrow, I find my way,
In this woven journey, I choose to stay.

Embracing myself, the tapestry thrives,
Crafted with journeys of countless lives.
In every layer, a truth to see,
A beautiful story—this is me.

Singing the Songs of My Heart

In the stillness, a melody grows,
Soft whispers rise, where passion flows.
Each note a feeling, a truth to share,
In the song of my heart, I lay bare.

Chords of laughter weave through the air,
A harmony born from love and care.
With every chorus, I feel alive,
Singing the songs that help me thrive.

Mornings greet me with radiant sound,
The sun shines bright as my dreams abound.
In the quiet, I find my voice,
In the rhythm of life, I rejoice.

Melodies linger in twilight's glow,
Each refrain a moment, a chance to grow.
From the depths of silence, I rise anew,
In the songs of my heart, I find the true.

With every breath, I sing my truth,
A serenade of life and youth.
In the symphony of tomorrow's start,
I embrace the songs that fill my heart.

Grounded in My Own Soil

Roots dig deep, where the heart can bloom,
In the richness of earth, I find my room.
Each layer whispers, ancient and wise,
Grounded in soil, beneath vast skies.

Vibrant life pulses beneath my feet,
In the warmth of the sun, I feel complete.
Nurtured by dreams that sprawl and grow,
In the garden of me, I'm blessed to know.

The seasons change, yet I stand tall,
Through storms and sun, I embrace it all.
In the silence, the seeds are sown,
Grounded in soil, I am never alone.

With every breath, I taste the earth,
Finding my purpose, my sense of worth.
In nature's embrace, I learn to be,
Grounded in soil, wild and free.

As the world spins on, I hold my space,
In the timeless dance, my sacred place.
With open arms, I fiercely sow,
Grounded in my own soil, I grow.

Beneath the Mask I Shed

Behind my smile, a silent ache,
Layers hidden, fears awake.
In shadows deep, I find the light,
A new beginning, a daring flight.

With each tear, I peel away,
What once was safe, what kept at bay.
Beneath the mask, I dare to dream,
Reclaim my being, let my heart beam.

Voices whisper, doubts take shape,
Yet still I rise, I find escape.
The courage blooms, within my chest,
Each breath I take, a quiet quest.

Embracing pain, I take control,
Fragments scattered, but still I'm whole.
With every step, I forge my way,
A stronger self, come what may.

No longer bound by expectations,
I live for me, my own creations.
Beneath the mask, the truth I find,
A fearless heart, a boundless mind.

Rising from the Ashes of Self-Doubt

In the depths where shadows creep,
My heart was lost, my dreams fell steep.
But from the wreckage, hope takes flight,
A spark ignites, a guiding light.

I gather strength from every scar,
Remind myself just who we are.
With each setback, I rise anew,
The ashes fade, revealing blue.

Resilience blooms within my soul,
I journey forth, I find my role.
The weight of doubt, I cast away,
With courage, I embrace the day.

Each step I take, a dance with fate,
No more the chains that silence hate.
Daring to dream, I break the mold,
A warrior's heart, fierce and bold.

So watch me rise, from dark to dawn,
A phoenix strong, forever drawn.
With every breath, I claim my worth,
A life reborn, a second birth.

Embracing the Unraveled

Threads of life, both frayed and worn,
In my chaos, a new dawn is born.
With open arms, I greet the tears,
Embracing moments, facing fears.

The tapestry of joy and pain,
Each unraveling, a diamond rain.
In each loose end, a chance to be,
Whole within this mystery.

Fingers crossed, I weave anew,
Fabric rich with every hue.
Each snag a story, each knot a need,
In the unraveling, I am freed.

No more the need for perfect seams,
I've found the grace in shattered dreams.
With every flaw, I come to see,
Beauty lies in raw honesty.

So take my heart, in pieces strewn,
I'll gather light, beneath the moon.
Embracing all that life has bared,
In every thread, my truth declared.

The Journey Back to Wholeness

A winding path, through tangled trees,
Whispers carried on a gentle breeze.
Each step a search for who I am,
To mend the heart, to learn to stand.

Fragments lost in the depths of time,
I gather pieces, start to climb.
With every stumble, lessons learned,
In quiet moments, bridges burned.

The road is long, yet so I find,
Rekindled strength within my mind.
In every shadow, light will glow,
The path unfolds, it starts to flow.

Hope is the compass that guides my way,
Through darkest nights and brightest day.
With open arms, I greet my fate,
Each passing doubt, I learn to shake.

The journey back, a sacred quest,
To find my peace, to give my best.
In every step, I dance with grace,
Returning, true, to my own embrace.

Finding Balance in Chaos

In restless winds, we stand our ground,
Amidst the noise, a peace is found.
The storm may roar, yet we remain,
With quiet strength, we bear the strain.

In fleeting moments, stillness calls,
A dance with shadows, the heart enthralls.
We breathe the chaos, find the grace,
In tumult's arms, we found our space.

With every drop of rain that falls,
We learn to rise, to stand, to crawl.
In fractured worlds, we seek the light,
A flicker in the endless night.

The balance found in every sway,
A gentle push to guide the way.
In chaos, life invites the flow,
With open hearts, we learn to grow.

So let the winds of change caress,
And in the dance, we find our rest.
In every storm, a strength unmasked,
In chaos, peace is found at last.

Rediscovering the Heartbeat

In silence deep, where echoes play,
I search for truths that fade away.
With every breath, I feel the spark,
A rhythm lost within the dark.

The pulse of life, a gentle hum,
Calls me back to where I'm from.
Through winding paths and shadows cast,
I reclaim the beats of my past.

Memories swirl like autumn leaves,
In every loss, a heart believes.
The whispers soft, the dreams take flight,
Rekindled hopes that ignite the night.

With open arms, I greet the dawn,
In tender moments, I am reborn.
In every heartbeat, love resides,
A symphony where truth abides.

So let me dance to this sweet sound,
In every silence, my soul is found.
Together we weave a world anew,
In rediscovery, my heart breaks through.

Portrait of the Authentic Self

In colors bright, my story flows,
A canvas bold, the journey shows.
Each stroke a tale, a moment's grace,
An honest glance, my truest face.

With shadows deep, the light reveals,
A tapestry of how it feels.
Each thread entwined, both light and dark,
In every eye, we leave our mark.

The art of living, messy yet true,
In every stumble, I find the hue.
A portrait forged from truths untold,
In vulnerability, we break the mold.

With every laugh, each tear that falls,
We craft the echoes of our calls.
In witnessing my heartache's worth,
I paint the beauty of my birth.

So let the colors blend and sway,
In authenticity, I find my way.
A portrait rich, forever spun,
In the gallery of who I've become.

Mosaic of My Journey

Each shard of glass, a fragment bright,
Reflects the moments, day and night.
With pieces scattered far and wide,
I weave my tale, I am the guide.

From trials faced to joys embraced,
In every turn, my dreams are traced.
With every crack, a story blooms,
In every space, a whisper looms.

The colors blend, both dark and light,
A mosaic formed in shadow's sight.
Through every storm, I've learned to see,
The beauty found in what can be.

With open heart, I find my place,
In life's mosaic, I leave my trace.
Each piece a journey, unique and true,
A story told in every hue.

So let the pieces fall and fit,
In chaos, beauty finds its wit.
Each step I take, a dance of chance,
In this mosaic, I find my stance.

Unveiling the Inner Light

In the quiet dawn of day,
Whispers of truth softly play.
Shadows retreat, fears take flight,
Hearts awaken to inner light.

Beneath the skin, a spark ignites,
Guiding shadows into the nights.
The soul's canvas begins to gleam,
As dreams emerge from the stream.

Each breath brings a melody new,
Colors blend, as if they knew.
With faith as the brush, love the hue,
Art of the heart, forever true.

Unraveled layers, tender threads,
Revealing paths where silence treads.
The mirror reflects, a sacred sight,
Transformation in the golden light.

Glimmers of hope, like stars align,
Every heartbeat, a sacred sign.
Through the veil, the spirit takes flight,
Embracing the power of inner light.

Journey to the Forgotten Self

Through tangled woods, old stories call,
In whispered tones, I hear them all.
Footsteps echo on paths unseen,
Leading me to where I've been.

Beneath the weight of time and space,
A hidden truth, a familiar face.
Memories dance like flickering flame,
Inviting me back to reclaim my name.

With open heart, I dare to seek,
Past what's strong, and what is weak.
Fragments of self long left behind,
In shadows cast, new light I'll find.

Each step forward, a stitch in time,
A melody lost now starts to chime.
In the stillness, the voice does swell,
On this journey, I know myself well.

Rivers of dawn and dusk intertwine,
In their embrace, memories align.
Every twist of fate, a lesson learned,
On the path where my spirit's burned.

From the ashes of doubt, I arise,
Seeing the world through unclouded eyes.
Into the light, the shadows fade,
I journey forth, no longer afraid.

Rebirth in Silent Echoes

In the hush of twilight's sigh,
Cloaked in dreams, I learn to fly.
Echoes cradle my weary heart,
In silence, I find a brand new start.

Beneath the weight of days gone by,
Whispers of hope, a gentle cry.
From ashes cold, new flames arise,
Transforming fate, beneath the skies.

Time holds secrets, soft and deep,
In silent echoes, the past will weep.
Yet through the tears, a vision clear,
Rebirth comes with every fear.

The cycle spins, like seasons do,
In nature's dance, the soul breaks through.
With every heartbeat, I reclaim,
The pieces lost, the spirit's flame.

In mirrored depth, the truth shall bloom,
From quietude emerges room.
Healing whispers where shadows roam,
In silent echoes, I find my home.

Charting Unfamiliar Waters

Set sail on the sea of dreams,
Where the horizon's light still gleams.
Waves of doubt may crash and roll,
Yet within, I hear the call of soul.

With each tide, I learn to steer,
Navigating through joy and fear.
The compass made from hope and grace,
Guides me forward, to embrace.

Clouds may linger; storms may rise,
But the heart knows to seek the skies.
Gentle breezes whisper true,
Charting courses, both fresh and new.

Among the swells, the stars align,
Each constellation, a sacred sign.
Through unfamiliar realms I roam,
This vast expanse, my heart's own home.

Finding treasures in every wave,
Lessons learned through the bold and brave.
In these waters, I'm never lost,
Embracing every wave, no matter the cost.